My Religion and Me

We are
BUDDHIST

Philip Blake

W
FRANKLIN WATTS
LONDON·SYDNEY

Franklin Watts
Published in Great Britain in 2015 by The Watts Publishing Group

Series designed and created for Franklin Watts by Storeybooks.

Acknowledgements
The Publisher would like to thank Liam, Need, Sonny and Thai for their help in
producing this book.
Faith advisor: Munisha, Education Officer, The Clear Vision Trust, www.clear-vision.org.

Photo credits:
Georgios Kollidas/Dreamstime: front cover bl .© Danita Delimont / Alamy pp 25 and 26;
I stock pp4, 5, 11, 13, 24 and 31. Additional photographs were supplied by the children
featured in the book, which despite their best efforts may not always be of the highest
quality. Every attempt has been made to clear copyright. Should there be any
inadvertent omission please apply to the publisher for rectification.

Dewey number: 294.3

ISBN: 978 1 4451 3891 6

Printed in Malaysia

Franklin Watts
An imprint of
Hachette Children's Group
Part of The Watts Publishing Group
Carmelite House
50 Victoria Embankment
London EC4Y 0DZ

An Hachette UK Company
www.hachette.co.uk

www.franklinwatts.co.uk

Note:
The opinions expressed in this book are personal to the children
we talked to and all opinions are subjective and can vary.

Contents

Words in **bold** can be found in the glossary

What is Buddhism?

▲ In Tibet, many boys start their education at a Buddhist **monastery** as young **monks**.

This statue of the ▶ Buddha shows him meditating with his legs crossed in the lotus position.

Buddhists follow the teachings of the great spiritual leader Siddhartha Gautama, known as the Buddha (a title that means 'the enlightened one'). Buddhism does not involve belief in a god. Buddhists believe the Buddha was a human being who reached perfect wisdom and compasson – a state called enlightenment. Having discovered the cause of suffering, he spent the rest of his life teaching others how they too could free themselves from suffering, and move towards enlightenment.

Karma

The Buddha taught that everything we do, think and say has a consequence, or result. Kind actions have positive results; selfishness and unkindness result in unhappiness. It matters how we behave because we and others will experience the consequences sooner or later, day by day and in future lives. This law of cause and effect is called the law of **karma**. Only kindness and wisdom will lead us towards enlightenment.

◀ *The Great **Stupa** at Sanchi, India, is one of the oldest Buddhist shrines. It was first built in the 3rd century BCE to hold relics of the Buddha.*

Living well

Buddhists aim to live kindly and wisely. Two important aids to doing this are studying the Buddha's teachings and meditating. **Meditation** is a way of stilling the mind so that it becomes more peaceful and more aware. Buddhism encourages people to take responsibility for their actions (karma), so Buddhists try to develop a loving heart towards living beings and the environment, to avoid causing harm.

*These two monks are praying at the Buddha Pagoda, an important Buddhist **shrine** in Bangkok, Thailand.* ▶

Buddhism Around the World

Buddhism began in northern India, and in the centuries after the Buddha's death it spread eastwards to countries such as China, Tibet and Japan.

There are still many Buddhists in these countries, as well as in Southeast Asia, where Buddhism is the national religion of Thailand. Most Southeast Asian Buddhists follow the kind of Buddhism called Theravada Buddhism, which stays closest to the Buddha's original teachings. People in China, Japan, and other parts of northern Asia, follow the group of traditions called Mahayana Buddhism. Lots of people in the rest of the world have also discovered the Buddha's teachings and are keen followers of his ideas. There are many people in the USA and Europe, as well as in countries such as Australia, who follow the different branches of Buddhism.

My name is Thai and I live in Brooklyn, New York, with my mom and dad. I am 11 years old and I am in grade five in a public school. I like to sing and dance and to write fiction. Each month we meet with other Buddhist families to meditate and talk about things such as **compassion**, kindness, and how to live more peaceful lives. That is important, especially in a non-stop city like New York.

My name is Liam and I live in Brighton in England. I am 11 years old and I have an older sister. I go to a local junior school and my hobbies are football, playing bass guitar and drama. I have a guinea pig named Toddles and my favourite subjects at school are science, maths, PE and art.

My name is Need and I am 11 years old. I live in Thailand, a country in Southeast Asia where Buddhism is the main religion. I am an only child. My hobbies are reading, writing journals, Taekwando, tennis, and horse-riding. I also like music and play the piano and the ranad, a Thai musical instrument.

I am Sonny and I'm 12 years old. I have a sister who is 15. I live in a Buddhist **community** in Australia and go to Kyogle High School. I like playing my drum kit and riding my bike.

In this book, four children share their experiences of Buddhist faith. It is important to remember that other Buddhists will have different opinions and experiences of their own faith.

7

A Buddhist Life
Liam's story

▲ *I am sitting comfortably, ready to begin meditation.*

Leading a Buddhist life means following the teachings of the Buddha, the great spiritual leader who lived in the 5th century BCE. We believe the Buddha was very special because he was the first person of his time to show people real compassion and to discover the true cause of suffering in the world.

The Buddha's enlightenment

After a long search for the truth about life and suffering, the Buddha achieved a state called enlightenment. This means that he was able to understand the true meaning of life, something that set him apart from other human beings of his time.

Thai says:
The Buddha taught that you don't have to be holy or super-smart to be free from suffering. We can all be more at peace.

A better life

As a Buddhist, I learn all about the Buddha's teachings, especially how he taught his followers the way to lead a better life by following a series of instructions called the **Eightfold Path**. The Path affects everything we do, and reduces the amount of suffering in our lives.

Great teachers

As well as the Buddha himself, Buddhists are guided by other notable teachers. In our family, we follow Tibetan Buddhism and our teacher is Sakyong Mipham **Rinpoche**, a great Tibetan spiritual leader who is also head of many monasteries and **retreat** centres around the world. We also pay special attention to the words of the Dalai Lama, the spiritual leader of the **Geluk school** of Tibetan Buddhism.

Need says:
I learn a lot about what the Buddha said and the kind of behaviour that helps us live a good life by taking part in chants about his teachings.

Sonny says:
To me Buddhism is not a religion, as there is no God. It is more like a way of life.

▼ *We meditate and listen to teachings at Buddhist centres, such as this one in Australia.*

The Buddha
Thai's story

The Buddha's original name was Siddhartha Gautama and he was the prince of a royal family in a town called Lumbini, which used to be in India but is now in Nepal. When he was young, his father kept his son inside the palace grounds, and did not allow him to travel where he might see old or sick people or other disturbing sights.

▲ *I am reading a book about Prince Siddhartha, who became the Buddha.*

An encounter with suffering

Eventually, Siddhartha went on a journey outside the palace and he was surprised how much sadness and pain there was in the world. When he saw the sick, the old and the poor, he was shocked and moved by their suffering.

The search for an answer

Siddhartha decided to see if he could discover a way to end suffering for everyone. At first, he thought that if you avoided all pleasures, like eating and enjoying yourself, you would reach enlightenment. But soon he saw that this only brought more pain for himself. But he realised that living a life of comfort and enjoyment would lead to pain too. The answer lay somewhere between these extremes, in the Middle Path.

The Buddha begins to teach

After a long time meditating, the Buddha reached enlightenment. At first, he thought he would not teach what he had learned, because the effort to reach enlightenment was so great that no one would want to learn his teachings. But later he decided to teach five followers and preached his first sermon in the Deer Park in Varanasi, the holiest city of ancient India.

Need says:
The Buddha and his teachings are described in the words of many of our chants.

◀ *Images of the Buddha often show him teaching. His thumb and finger make a circle, standing for the '**Wheel of the Law**', a term for his teachings.*

11

The Eightfold Path
Thai's story

▲ *Discussing Buddhism with my friends is an important part of my faith.*

In his first sermon, the Buddha spoke about the Four Noble Truths. The first truth is that life involves suffering, the second that the cause of suffering is desire, the third is that suffering can be ended, and the fourth that the way to end suffering is to follow the Eightfold Path. Like all Buddhists, I try hard to follow the Eightfold Path in everything I do.

Following the Path
The Eightfold Path covers eight of the most important things in our lives, from the way we think and speak, through our

◄ This symbol on the roof of a temple in Lhasa, Tibet, shows the 'Wheel of the Dharma'. It has eight spokes, which stand for the Eightfold Path.

actions and work, to the way we concentrate and meditate. By following the Eightfold Path, a person reduces the amount of suffering he or she experiences by living a life of virtue. For example, people who live the Eightfold Path tend to speak well of others and do not engage in rumours or gossip. They tend to choose jobs that help other people, and they usually think positively about many aspects of life, including about other people, animals and the world as a whole.

Liam says:
Because he reached enlightenment, the Buddha was able to teach us how to follow the Eightfold Path in our everyday lives.

The path
The Eightfold Path covers these parts of our lives:

Correct understanding
Correct thoughts
Correct speech
Correct conduct or action
Correct livelihood or job
Correct effort
Correct mindfulness or awareness
Correct concentration

How the Path helps me
Now that I follow the Eightfold Path, I eat more mindfully, taking my time and appreciating the flavours, focusing on what I'm eating and being grateful for the gift of food. I am also more relaxed, which means that I can learn better, both in and out of school.

The Triple Refuge
Liam's story

"

One ceremony that many Buddhists perform is called the Triple Refuge. This is a special ritual during which we say the words, "I take refuge in the Buddha, the Dharma and the Sangha."

The Dharma means the teachings of the Buddhist path and the Sangha is the community of other Buddhists who support us and help us to be compassionate and patient in our daily lives.

Performing the Triple Refuge

Although we do not perform the Triple Refuge every day in our family, we try to do so often. The Triple Refuge is a way of showing our **devotion** to the Buddha, his teaching, and the Buddhist community, and of contemplating the meaning of these things in our faith. When performing the Triple Refuge, Buddhists try to think about the

▲ *We offer water and **incense** at our home shrine.*

meaning of the words – especially to remember how the Buddha's teaching helps us to clarify our point of view and to live a better life. There is a special booklet that we read from, which helps guide us when we do the Triple Refuge.

Respect for the Buddha

In our home there are several images of the Buddha. They are an inspiration to us and a sign of our devotion to the Buddha. To show our respect we always treat these statues carefully, and place them quite high in the room. On our home shrine are a statue of the Buddha, water bowls, which stand for generosity, candles, which represent a clear mind, and a crystal sphere, which stands for a pure mind. There are also pictures of the leaders of Shambala Buddhism, the kind of Buddhism we practise.

▲ *We also do a more elaborate version of the Triple Refuge ceremony when we become full members of the Buddhist community. At my sister's ceremony, a small lock of her hair was cut and she was given her special Buddhist name, Sangye Lhamo, which means Buddha Goddess.*

The five water bowls on our shrine at home represent generosity. The candles represent a clear mind. ▶

Family Sittings
Liam's story

▲ *I begin a Family Sitting by showing my devotion to the Buddha at our family shrine at home.*

Twice a week I get together with my parents and my sister and we have a Family Sitting at home. The main activity in a Family Sitting is meditation, but it is also a time when we can discuss our lives together.

Calming the mind
At the Family Sitting we talk about what has happened during the day and meditate for about five minutes.

The Sitting helps us to calm down if annoying things have happened to us, helping us to clear our minds and relax.

Beginning the Sitting

Our shrine is normally closed, but at the beginning of a Family Sitting, we open the shrine and bow to the Buddha to show our respect for him and our devotion. Then we each sit on a meditation cushion and prepare for meditation by relaxing and focusing on our breathing.

Right Mindfulness

Meditation especially helps me to follow the seventh part of the Eightfold Path, which is concerned with Right **Mindfulness**. It enables me to develop a kind and happy mind. I find that meditation is a really important part of my life – both in helping me to be happy and in making it easier to concentrate on whatever I am doing. I also meditate when taking part in a Youth Meditation Programme and at Family Camp at our retreat centre.

Sonny says:
When people visit our community, some come for teaching ceremonies, but others come for long retreats that can last up to three years.

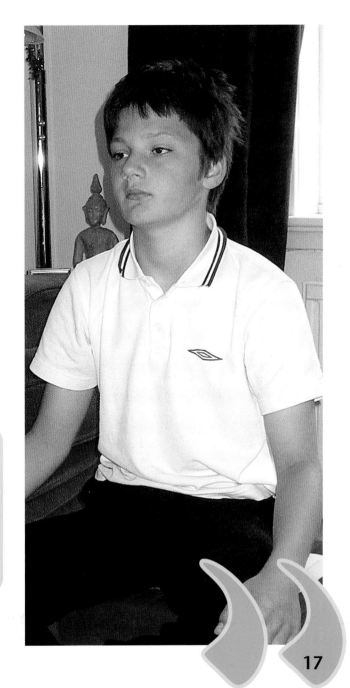

Need says:
When I catch my mind wandering during meditation, I try to concentrate on my breathing to empty my mind of distracting thoughts.

I prepare to meditate and clear my ▶ *mind of distracting thoughts.*

My Community
Sonny's story

◄ With some of my friends I took part in a workshop with a Buddhist rap artist called Karuna.

I live with my parents and my sister in a Buddhist community. I have plenty of Buddhist friends amongst the other people in the community and also enjoy the chance to meet Buddhists from all over the world who come to our gompa (meditation centre).

Friends and neighbours

Our community is on about 800 acres of land that is mostly covered in sub-tropical rainforest. There are 14 people who live here in houses that are about

Thai says:
Buddhism is still quite new in New York so there are lots of adult meditators, but very few kids. I hope that our community continues to grow.

▲ *At our gompa there is a shrine with a large image of the Buddha, a cupboard with lots of Buddhist books and benches where we can sit to listen to the teachings.*

one kilometre apart. It is good to have friends nearby – I can drop in on our neighbours at any time and they are more like family than friends.

Animal visitors

We have a rule in the community that we must not harm animals, so lots of tame wildlife visits our garden. Creatures such as wallabies, koalas, parrots and goanas (two-metre-long lizards) visit us, and friendly pythons come to our back verandah. We also have a spring-fed creek (stream) that we can swim in.

▲ *I have made friends with one of the wallabies who visits our garden.*

Buddhists from overseas

It's good meeting all the people who come from all around the world to our meditation centre. People come from as far away as Canada, Brazil, Britain and India. Everyone is very friendly and it is interesting meeting them all because they all have very different experiences. Some of them have become special friends.

Our Teacher
Sonny's story

▲ *Some of my overseas friends are from Mongolia. They showed me how to ride a camel!*

All the people in our community are inspired by our main teacher, Dzongsar Khyentse Rinpoche. We look forward to his visits to our community, which usually take place once or twice every year.

A great teacher

Dzongsar Khyentse Rinpoche was born in Bhutan. Like many Buddhist teachers, he spent his childhood in a monastery, where he studied Buddhism. He has set up several centres for Buddhist learning and retreats all over the world, from North America to the Far East.

In Australia

Dzongsar Khyentse Rinpoche is abbot (or leader) of our meditation centre, but he is not a monk. We all value his teachings highly – his title, Rinpoche, means 'precious **guru**'. He is a very kind person, and very wise, but he also likes to play tricks on people, for example, he gave us chocolate but it had chilli in it and it was really spicy!

> *Need says:*
> My understanding of Buddhism is helped by listening to talks given by our monk teacher.

Yearly teachings

In our teacher's annual lessons, he spends a lot of time talking to us about many different Buddhist texts. He has written a number of books, so his followers can study his teachings when he is not present. He is also a film maker. He wrote and directed the films *The Cup* and *Travellers and Magicians*. He teaches through his films.

▼ *Our teacher Dzongsar Khyentse Rinpoche (centre) leads a ritual at our gompa. My sister, Tara, who is in the blue dress, is one of those taking part.*

On Retreat
Need's story

▲ *While I was on retreat I made a flower-garland to give to my parents to say thank you to them for all they do for me.*

Thai says:
I learn more about Buddhism by attending summer retreats with other Buddhist families.

Several times each year I go on retreat to learn more about Buddhism, to pay respect to the Buddha, the Dhamma, and the Sangha, and to meditate and clear my mind. I go either to Thawsi Scholl in Bangkok or to Ban-Boon, a big house whose owner provides it to be used as a retreat centre on two Sundays in each month. I usually go with my family, especially with my mom. The main things I do on retreat are chanting, meditation and listening to talks about the Dhamma.

Chanting
We chant to pay respect to the Buddha, the Dhamma and the Sangha, and to praise their high moral values. Some of our chants reflect and recall the Buddha's teachings, some recall actions that lead to a good and worthy life, some describe the core of the Buddha's teaching, and some enable us to share blessings.

Meditation

We take part in both sitting meditation, and in a kind of meditation that we do as we walk around. I usually meditate by concentrating on my own breath, clearing my mind as I breathe in and out. My mind stays focused for some time after each retreat. I become more mindful when doing my classes and homework, and calm myself more quickly if I become angry. The lessons about the Dhamma also help me in my daily life.

The Eight Precepts

The Buddha taught his monks eight habits or **precepts**. The precepts are followed today by Buddhist monks, but all of us follow them on retreat to help us concentrate less on ourselves and more on others. The Eight Precepts are:

Not harming living creatures
Not taking what is not given
Not taking part in any sexual acts
Not speaking incorrectly (lying)
Not taking drugs or alcohol
Not eating at wrong times (we have one meal a day on retreat)
Not taking part in dancing, music or plays, and not using self-adornment
Not using a high or luxurious bed

◀ ▼ *I have sitting and walking meditation three times a day when I am on retreat.*

23

Vesak

Need's story

▲ At Vesak people decorate statues of the Buddha as a child with flowers.

Thai says:
One story about the Buddha says that when he was born he started walking immediately and with every step he took, a lotus flower would bloom.

The full moon day of the sixth month of the lunar calendar is Visakha Bucha. It is also called Vesak or Wesak in some places. Vesak is the most famous Buddhist festival. It marks three really important events in the life of the Buddha – when he was born, when he achieved enlightenment and when he went to his death.

Celebrating Vesak
We believe that all these events happened on the same date in the calendar, and we celebrate in various different ways. In many parts of the world, people send each other cards, put up decorations or flags outside their houses and light candles.

▲ Lotus flower.

Offerings at the temple

Many people go to a temple or monastery to celebrate the festival. They take flowers, candles and **incense**, and offer these as a way of paying respect to the Triple Refuge of the Buddha, his Dhamma or teaching, and the Sangha or community of monks and other Buddhists.

The procession

When at the temple, people take part in a candle-lit procession. They walk around the temple three times, carrying a candle, flowers and sticks of incense as they walk. They go around three times, once for the Buddha, once for the Dhamma and once for the Sangha.

▼ *People gather outside a monastery to celebrate Vesak.*

My Vesak
Need's story

In my family at Vesak, we start the day with special chants and a meditation. Then we usually go to a monastery where we join other Buddhists and the monks, taking part in special chants and rituals in honour of the Buddha.

Vesak rituals

At the monastery during Vesak, the abbot or one of the monks gives a talk about the Dhamma to everyone who comes. Then we join him in a special chanting ceremony. After this, I take part in a candle-lit walking meditation.

◀ Lighting and carrying candles is one of the traditions of Vesak.

Helping others

The monastery allows me and my school-friends to bring food to give to all the people who come to the festival. Enjoying this food is a way of helping others while also having a good time.

Helping the planet

When we visit the monastery we also learn about recycling and ways in which we can reduce global warming – for example by reducing the rubbish we throw away and by making things from materials we recycle. We make things like baskets from used milk cartons. By doing this, we celebrate Vesak as a way of caring for the planet.

▼ *We meditate as we walk around the precinct of the monastery.*

Glossary

Buddha 'Enlightened One' The title given to Siddhartha Gautama, founder of Buddhism, and others who have reached the state of enlightenment.

community A group of people living together or sharing the same beliefs or culture.

compassion A feeling of kindness towards those who are suffering.

devotion Strong love or admiration for someone or something.

Dharma (or Dhamma) The teaching of the Buddha.

Eightfold Path The path or way of life that leads from suffering towards enlightenment.

enlightenment The state of complete spiritual awareness and knowledge of the meaning of life.

Geluk school One of the four main branches of Buddhism in Tibet.

gompa A monastery or spiritual centre where people can go to retreat, meditate, and hear Buddhist teachings.

guru A religious teacher, especially one with deep spiritual knowledge.

incense A substance, used in religious rituals, that gives off a fragrant smell when burned.

karma (or kamma) The teaching that all our actions have effects or consequences, and that these consequences affect our happiness day by day and in future lives.

lunar calendar The calendar based on the 28-day phases of the moon.

meditation A way of calming the mind and body, for example by focusing your attention on your breathing.

mindfulness A kindly, patient awareness of what you are doing, thinking and feeling and the people around you.

monastery A building that is home to a community of monks (or nuns).

monk A man who has devoted himself to meditation and study and chosen to live with other monks in a monastery, obeying a set of strict rules about the way he lives his life and relying on the wider Buddhist community for food and support.

precept An ethical guideline for living kindly and wisely.

retreat A period of time, usually spent in a special place away from home, during which people can meditate, listen to religious teachings, and spend quiet time in thought.

Rinpoche A title, meaning 'precious guru', given to revered Buddhist leaders and teachers in the Tibetan tradition.

Sangha The Buddhist community; sometimes the word Sangha is used to mean the community of Buddhist monks and nuns, sometimes all Buddhists.

shrine A special place where images of the Buddha are kept, acting as a focus for devotion.

Sitting A session during which people discuss religious matters and meditate together.

stupa A building, in the form of a domed structure or a tower, built to house relics or other sacred objects.

Triple Refuge The Buddha, Dharma (his teachings) and Sangha (community of Buddhists). It is also the name of a ritual in which Buddhists place their trust in these three precious things, which are also known as the Three Gems.

Vesak (or Wesak or Viskha Bucha) An important Buddhist festival, which marks the enlightenment of the Buddha. Some Buddhists also celebrate his birth and death on the same day.

Wheel of the Law A symbol in the form of a wheel with eight spokes, standing for the Eightfold Path. Also known as the Dharmachakra.

Further Information

Websites
BBC Religion and Ethics
www.bbc.co.uk/religion/religions/buddhism/

Buddhist Information and Education Network
http://buddhanet.net/

The Buddhist Society Resources
www.thebuddhistsociety.org/resources/index.html

Buddhist Festivals

There are Buddhists living all over the world and most of them use the calendars of the countries in which they live. But there are also traditional Buddhist calendars, which vary from one part of the world to another. These traditional calendars are mostly used to calculate the dates of religious festivals. They are lunar calendars, which means that they are based on the phases of the moon. Each month is 28 days in length.

Because the calendars vary a lot, and because there are different branches of Buddhism, Buddhist festivals vary greatly – some are celebrated only in Japan, others only in Tibet. Those, such as Vesak, that are celebrated in many places sometimes have different dates in different parts of the world.

Dharma Day
This festival celebrates the Buddha's first teaching of the Dharma, or the Truth. A few weeks after his enlightenment, he met again five old friends who were also looking for the

truth about life. He told them what he had discovered, about the cause of suffering and the way leading to enlightenment. As they listened, one by one they too became enlightened.

Losar
This is the New Year festival in Tibet. People clean their houses, put on new clothes, exchange gifts and pay visits to the monasteries, where they make offerings to the monks. This is also a time when people give to the poor.

Higan
The festival of Higan is celebrated in Japan twice a year, in the spring and autumn. As well as signalling changes in the seasons, these festivals are also linked to spiritual change, from the world of suffering to the state of enlightenment.

Hana Matsuri
Hana Matsuri is the festival at which Zen Buddhists, especially in Japan, celebrate the birthday of the Buddha. In temples, the monks wash the images of the Buddha in a special tea made from the leaves of the hydrangea plant.

Vesak
Also known as Visakha Bucha or Wesak, Vesak is the most important festival for many Buddhists. It marks the Buddha's birth, enlightenment and death. In Theravada countries such as Thailand and Sri Lanka, this festival is widely celebrated – people put up lanterns, take part in processions and other street entertainments, and visit the monasteries.

Poson
This festival commemorates the teacher Mahinda, who brought Buddhism to Sri Lanka. It is widely celebrated on the island, and events in Mahinda's life are acted out.

Index